Scribble Scrabble

To Hudson and Bennett,
for creating the first
scribble-scrabble stories.
Your creativity and
imagination inspire us all.

Scribble Scrabble

Written by: Amanda Shackelford

Illustrated by: Leslie Warner

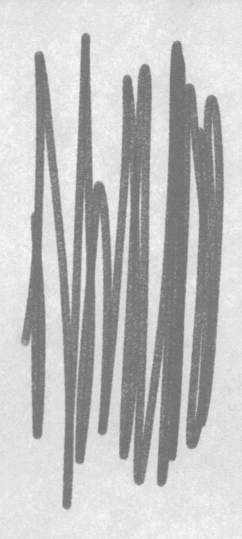

Scribbles can go up. Scribbles can go down.

Scribbles can go around and around.

A scribble can be squiggly, or it can be straight.

There are so many ways to draw lines.
Isn't that great?

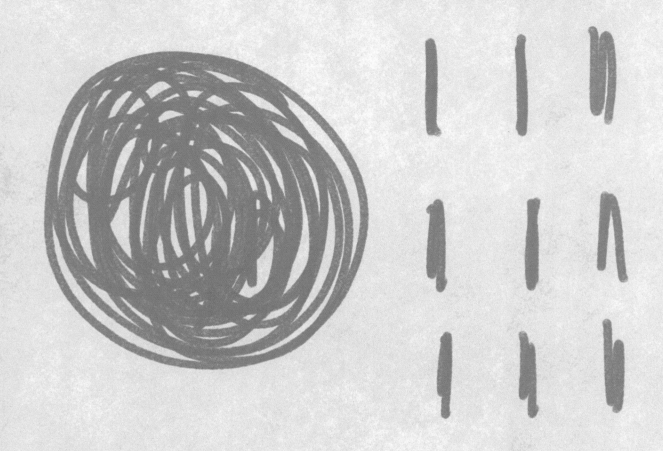

Scribbles can make circles and
scribbles can make lines.

With a splash of yellow, you've got
a sun that shines.

Grab a green crayon and scribble up, scribble down. Now you have grass covering the ground!

Scribble brown up, scribble brown down. Add some green whirls, and you have trees all around!

Scribble red in a circle - it's okay to go slow. Add a brown line for the stem, and look how it's grown!

Draw a green line, then scribble with pink. Look at the flower you made in a blink!

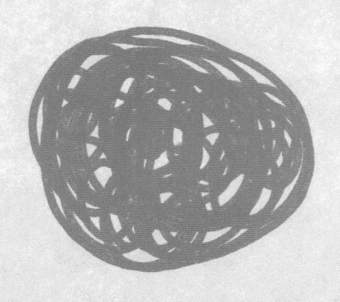

Want to scribble a person? Start with a scribble going around and around...

Add some arms, legs, and a face. Then you have a character, bringing life to the space!

Scribbles can just be scribbles,
plain as can be.

But with colors, they transform into art, you see!

You could scribble a house...

Or even a mouse!

You can use green to scribble a dinosaur, a creature from the past that we all adore!

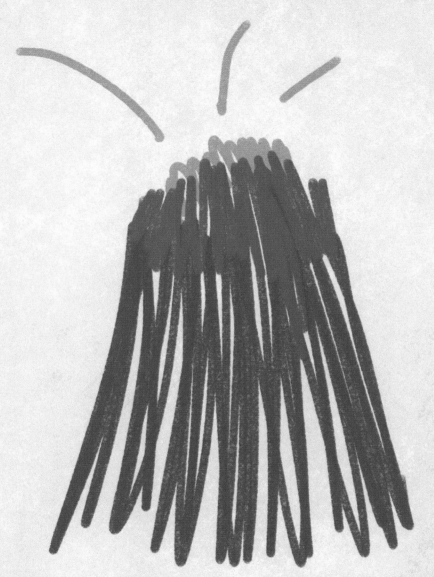

The top of a volcano can be a red scribble, with lava bubbling up in a fiery dribble.

A scribble could help a rocket blast off into space, zooming past stars in a thrilling race!

You could scribble a blue car or a
boat, bringing adventures to life with
each stroke!

So take a crayon and start to scribble
scrabble...

You'll never know what story will unravel!

Finish the Scribble

Can you help scribble in the lion's mane?

Finish the Scribble

Can you help the rocket blast off into space?

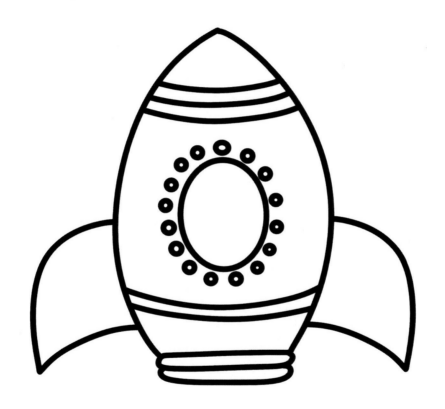

Draw your own scribble story

Draw your own scribble story

Did you know...

Before your child can learn to write letters, they need to be able to draw these shapes

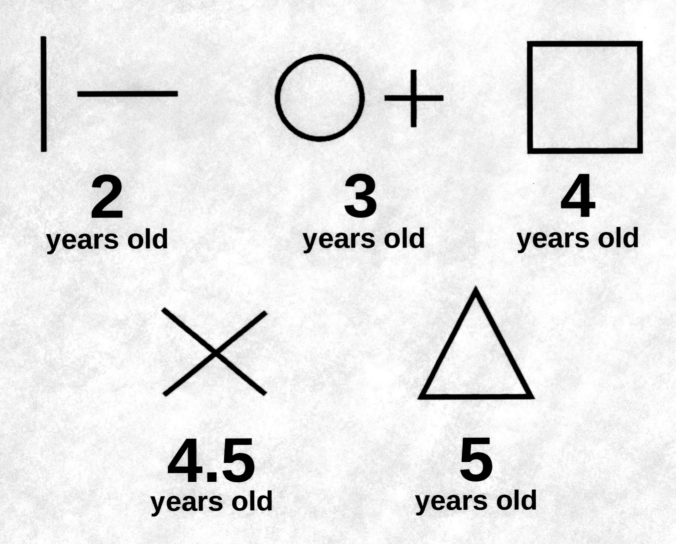

Drawing Stages

Random
Scribbling

Controlled
Scribbling

Lines and
Patterns

Pictures of
people/objects

Meet the author

Amanda is a former kindergarten teacher who now dedicates her expertise to developing writing curriculum for preschool, kindergarten, and first-grade students. When she isn't crafting curriculum for young learners, Amanda is chasing after her three little boys who inspire her to create new and engaging lessons.

Scan the QR code for more activities and lesson plans.
www.thatkindermama.com

Meet the illustrator

Leslie has been scribbling for 36 years and doesn't plan on stopping! She lives in Wisconsin with her husband & two sons. If she is on a break from scribbling, she's probably on a run.

Made in the USA
Coppell, TX
01 July 2025

51378539R00021